Uni Planner
Quarter System Edition

Table of Contents

♡ self-love ⌒ reflection ⚖ balance ⦙ health
⏱ time management ⚆ achievement ▦ study aid

ii

Preface

Dear Student,

I care about your college experience. I care that you are in your best state: physically, mentally, and socially. I want you to avoid suffering and I want you to succeed. It breaks my heart when my friend or acquaintance is so overwhelmed and busy that he/she is skipping meals or sleeping very little. This planner was designed with myself, my friends, and all the college students I've met in mind. I too have been guilty of putting my health second to schoolwork and other responsibilities. This planner is designed to help you recognize bad habits, combat worries and stress, and take care of yourself so you can optimize your results for this quarter. It will help you stay organized and motivated through the toughest times of the quarter. It will remind you to squeeze in personal time for leisure and self growth, because no matter how busy or committed we are to school, we can't lose sense of ourselves. It will help you to realize your full potential, because that's what you deserve.

I've included spaces on worksheets for 8 courses, not because I think it's a usual number to take, but because I want to accommodate everyone. If you only have 4 courses, you can use these additional spaces to keep track of research responsibilities, club responsibilities and deadlines, and recreational classes.

Many aspects of this planner can be taken as suggestions. Journal prompts are food for thought, and usage of this planner is meant to be extremely flexible. I've tried my best to make prompts appropriate for each day of the quarter, but ultimately you should use what you find helpful. There are many specific features as well as ample blank space, so use this planner to your liking.

The 3 week overviews are designed to let you glance at what's ahead and only worry about the near future. You may fill them out at the beginning or as you go through the quarter. When you're filling out a weekly overview, you may go to the day-page to-do lists and schedule in tasks. At the end of the week, you can return to the weekly overview page to reflect on your progress.

Because self-love is so important for moving forward from mistakes and not giving up, I've dedicated Week 0 journal entries to promoting self-love and confidence before the new quarter starts. I suggest that you work through these sections to put yourself on a great path.

I wish you the best this quarter!

Sincerely,
Uni Planner

Class Schedule

All the essentials in one place. Record classes & meetings, library hours & printing, store hours, etc.

	Monday	Tuesday	Wednesday
7:00			
7:30			
8:00			
8:30			
9:00			
9:30			
10:00			
10:30			
11:00			
11:30			
12:00			
12:30			
1:00			
1:30			
2:00			
2:30			
3:00			
3:30			
4:00			
4:30			
5:00			
5:30			
6:00			
6:30			
7:00			
7:30			

Course	Lecture Office Hours	Discussion/Lab Office Hours

Thursday	Friday	Notes

Location	Hours	Notes

Grade Composition

Record %s, track scores, attendance, etc.
Use blank gray boxes for other items.

Course	Participation	Homework	Quizzes
Grade/Notes			
Grade/Notes			
Grade/Notes			
Grade/Notes			
Grade/Notes			
Grade/Notes			
Grade/Notes			
Grade/Notes			

Papers	Midterms	Final		

Course Reading List

	Course 1	Course 2
Week 0 M/T		
W/R		
F		
Week 1 M/T		
W/R		
F		
Week 2 M/T		
W/R		
F		
Week 3 M/T		
W/R		
F		
Week 4 M/T		
W/R		
F		
Week 5 M/T		
W/R		
F		

Course 3	Course 4

Course Reading List

	Course 5	Course 6
Week 0 M/T		
W/R		
F		
Week 1 M/T		
W/R		
F		
Week 2 M/T		
W/R		
F		
Week 3 M/T		
W/R		
F		
Week 4 M/T		
W/R		
F		
Week 5 M/T		
W/R		
F		

8

Course 7	Course 8

Course Reading List

	Course 1	Course 2
Week 6 M/T		
W/R		
F		
Week 7 M/T		
W/R		
F		
Week 8 M/T		
W/R		
F		
Week 9 M/T		
W/R		
F		
Week 10 M/T		
W/R		
F		
Deadweek M/T		
W/R		
F		

Course 3	Course 4

Course Reading List

Week 6 - 10 & Deadweek (if applicable) for Courses 5 - 8

	Course 5	Course 6
Week 6 M/T		
W/R		
F		
Week 7 M/T		
W/R		
F		
Week 8 M/T		
W/R		
F		
Week 9 M/T		
W/R		
F		
Week 10 M/T		
W/R		
F		
Deadweek M/T		
W/R		
F		

12

Course 7	Course 8

Course of Action

To be done before classes start. Evaluation of expectations, and plan for success.

Course	Comfort Level	Worries about Class

Strengths	Time Dedication	Course of Action

Reward System

Treat yourself, not just when you remember to, but because you deserve it regularly

Scheduled Personal Time

Reward Yourself Periodically

Time	Thoughts	Actions
after each day		
after each week		
after each month		
after a stressful day		
after each deadline		
after each exam		

Celebrating Accomplishments

Reward Each Small Step & Every Big One

Accomplishment	Thoughts	Actions
achieving a goal		
accomplishing something I didn't think I could do		
finishing something boring/tedious		
finishing a long project		
successfully pulling an all-nighter		

Recharge

Brainstorm how to celebrate positive emotions, and how to recover from negative ones

Positive Emotions — *Don't overlook the positives*

Emotion	Thoughts	Actions
proud		
confident		
fulfilled		
accomplished		
helpful		

Negative Emotions — *Brainstorm ways to rethink & react better to situations*

Emotion	Thoughts	Actions
Disappointed		
Self-Doubting or Self-Critical		
Frustrated		
Insecure		
Unmotivated		

Week 0 - 2	The Big Day(s)

Week Goals	Monday	Tuesday	Wednesday
Week 0			
Anticipated Stress	○ ○ ○ ○ ○	○ ○ ○ ○ ○	○ ○ ○ ○ ○
Week 1			
Anticipated Stress	○ ○ ○ ○ ○	○ ○ ○ ○ ○	○ ○ ○ ○ ○
Week 2			
Anticipated Stress	○ ○ ○ ○ ○	○ ○ ○ ○ ○	○ ○ ○ ○ ○

Stressful Days	The Day Before	The Week Before

Inspiration From Myself	Inspiration From Others

Focus on what's right in front of you. Set goals in advance.
Anticipate stress & plan ways to combat. Seek inspiration & maintain
motivation. Keep track of projects and progress.

Thursday	Friday	Saturday	Sunday

○ ○ ○ ○ ○   ○ ○ ○ ○ ○ ○   ○ ○ ○ ○ ○   ○ ○ ○ ○ ○ ○

○ ○ ○ ○ ○   ○ ○ ○ ○ ○ ○   ○ ○ ○ ○ ○   ○ ○ ○ ○ ○ ○

○ ○ ○ ○ ○   ○ ○ ○ ○ ○ ○   ○ ○ ○ ○ ○   ○ ○ ○ ○ ○ ○

Main Projects	Steps	Progress/Reflection

My Notes

Week 0

/ - /

	Monday	Tuesday	Wednesday
Deadlines			
Events/Meetings			
Meals	☐ B ☐ L ☐ D	☐ B ☐ L ☐ D	☐ B ☐ L ☐ D
Exercise			

Goals	Plan of Action	Result/Reflection

Academic Habits	M	T	W	R	F	S	S	Personal Habits	M	T	W	R	F	S	S

How I Feel About My Classes? *1 Nervous* *2 Ready* *3 Confident* 20

Course 1 ☐☐☐   Course 2 ☐☐☐   Course 3 ☐☐☐   Course 4 ☐☐☐
Course 5 ☐☐☐   Course 6 ☐☐☐   Course 7 ☐☐☐   Course 8 ☐☐☐

Thursday

Friday

Saturday

Sunday

☐ B
☐ L
☐ D

☐ B
☐ L
☐ D

☐ B
☐ L
☐ D

☐ B
☐ L
☐ D

Academic	Extracurricular	Personal	Priorities

My Notes

Monday

Today's Mantra for ___ / ___ / ___

Sleep _____ hrs

Mood _____

Caffeine _____ servings

Worries About the Quarter

Enthusiasms for the Quarter

Fun Things To Do Before Quarter "Starts"

My Thoughts

Rate My Day _____

Mood _____

Stress Level _____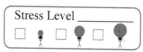

Prepare for School

School Supplies

Food/Snacks

Errands

Shopping List

Prepare Myself

Social Time

Personal Time

Errands

Reminders

My Notes

Tuesday

Today's Mantra for ___/___/___

Sleep _____ hrs

Mood _____

Caffeine _____ servings

Academic Strengths	New Outlets & Improvements
....	....
....	....
....	....
....	....
....	....
....	....
....	....
....	....

Academic Weaknesses	Reassurance & Improvements
....	....
....	....
....	....
....	....
....	....
....	....
....	....
....	....

My Thoughts

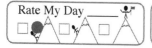

Rate My Day _____

Mood _____

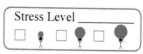

Stress Level _____

Today's Mission

Important Things

Prepare for School

Prepare Myself

Organize

For Confidence

Declutter

For Fun

Simplify

For Relaxation

Shopping List

Reminders

My Notes

Wednesday

Today's Mantra for   /   /

Sleep _____ hrs

Mood _____

Caffeine _____ servings

Personal Strengths

Praises & Improvements

Personal Weaknesses

Forgiveness & Improvements

My Thoughts

Rate My Day _____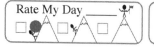

Mood _____

Stress Level _____

Today's Mission

Important Things

For School

Main Focus

Productive Breaks

Get Started

Get Ahead

For Myself

Main Focus

Stress-Free Tasks

Get Started

Personal Time

My Notes

Thursday

Today's Mantra for   /   /

Sleep _____ hrs

Mood _____

Caffeine _____ servings

What I Love About Myself Now	What I Can Learn to Love

Mind

Body

Soul

My Thoughts

Rate My Day _____

Mood _____

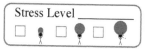

Stress Level _____

For School

Main Focus

Productive Breaks

Get Started

Get Ahead

For Myself

Main Focus

Stress-Free Tasks

Get Started

Personal Time

My Notes

Week 0

Friday

Today's Mantra for ___ / ___ / ___

Sleep _____ hrs

Mood _____

Caffeine _____ servings

Staying In: *Fun Things to Do This Quarter*

- [ ]
- [ ]
- [ ]
- [ ]
- [ ]
- [ ]
- [ ]
- [ ]

Going Out: *Fun Things to Do This Quarter*

- [ ]
- [ ]
- [ ]
- [ ]
- [ ]
- [ ]
- [ ]
- [ ]

My Thoughts

Rate My Day _____

Mood _____

Stress Level _____

Today's Mission

Important Things

30

For School

Priority This Weekend

Start This Weekend

I'm Feeling Productive

Get Ahead

For Myself

Weekend Errands

Social Time

Surprise Myself

Personal Time

My Notes

Saturday

Today's Mantra for   /   /

Sleep _____ hrs

Mood _____

Caffeine _____ servings

Good Memories This Week

....

....

....

....

....

....

....

....

Memories I Want to Make This Quarter

....

....

....

....

....

....

....

....

....

My Thoughts

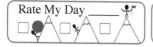

Rate My Day _____

Mood _____

Stress Level _____

For School

Start Easy

Catch Up On

Get Started On

Get Ahead

For Myself

For Confidence

For Fun

For Relaxation

Hobbies

My Notes

Week 0

Sunday

Today's Mantra for ___ / ___ / ___

Sleep _____ hrs

Mood _____

Caffeine ____ servings

Goals This Quarter	Why I Want These Goals
Academic	
....	....
....	....
....	....
....	....
....	....
Extracurricular	
....	....
....	....
....	....
....	....
....	....
Personal	
....	....
....	....
....	....
....	....
....	....

My Thoughts

Rate My Day _____

Mood _____

Stress Level _____

For School

Redeem Myself

To Feel Proud

Only If Possible

Get Ahead

For Myself

For Inspiration

For Positivity

For Self-Love

Hobbies

My Notes

Week 1

/ - /

Monday	Tuesday	Wednesday

Deadlines

Events/Meetings

Meals

Monday:
- [ ] B
- [ ] L
- [ ] D

Tuesday:
- [ ] B
- [ ] L
- [ ] D

Wednesday:
- [ ] B
- [ ] L
- [ ] D

Exercise

Goals	Plan of Action	Result/Reflection

Academic Habits	M	T	W	R	F	S	S

Personal Habits	M	T	W	R	F	S	S

How I Feel About My Classes? 1 *Behind* 2 *On Track* 3 *Ahead*

Course 1 [ ][ ][ ]   Course 2 [ ][ ][ ]   Course 3 [ ][ ][ ]   Course 4 [ ][ ][ ]

Course 5 [ ][ ][ ]   Course 6 [ ][ ][ ]   Course 7 [ ][ ][ ]   Course 8 [ ][ ][ ]

Thursday	Friday	Saturday
		Sunday

☐ B   ☐ L   ☐ D   ☐ B   ☐ L   ☐ D   ☐ B   ☐ L   ☐ D   ☐ B   ☐ L   ☐ D

Academic	Extracurricular	Personal	
			Priorities

My Notes

Week 1

Monday

Today's Mantra for ___ / ___ / ___

Sleep _____ hrs
☐ 👤 ☐ 👤 ☐ 👤💤

Mood _____
☐ 😞 ☐ 😐 ☐ 😊

Caffeine ____ servings
☐ ☕ ☐ ☕ ☐ 🥤

How I'm Going to Stay on Track This Quarter

Academic

....
....
....
....
....

Extracurricular

....
....
....
....
....

Mental Health

....
....
....
....
....

My Thoughts

Rate My Day _____
☐ ☐ ☐

Mood _____
☐ 😞 ☐ 😐 ☐ 😊

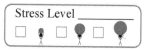
Stress Level _____
☐ ☐ ☐

Today's Mission

Important Things

For School

Main Focus

Productive Breaks

Get Started

For Myself

Main Focus

Smaller Tasks

Get Started

Study - Review - Prepare

Personal Time

My Notes

Week 1

Tuesday

Today's Mantra for / /

Sleep _____ hrs

Mood _____

Caffeine ____ servings

Mistakes I Made Last Quarter	Fixing Them This Quarter
....	....
....	....
....	....
....	....
....	....
....	....
....	....
....	....
....	....
....	....
....	....
....	....
....	....
....	....
....	....
....	....
....	....
....	....

My Thoughts

Rate My Day _____

Mood _____

Stress Level _____

Today's Mission

Important Things

For School

Main Focus

Productive Breaks

Get Started

Get Ahead

For Myself

Main Focus

Stress-Free Tasks

Get Started

Personal Time

My Notes

Wednesday

Today's Mantra for   /   /

Sleep _____ hrs

Mood _____

Caffeine _____ servings

Organizational Strengths	Room for Improvement

My Thoughts

Today's Mission

Important Things

For School

Main Focus

Productive Breaks

Get Started

Get Ahead

For Myself

Main Focus

Stress-Free Tasks

Get Started

Personal Time

My Notes

Week 1

Thursday

Today's Mantra for ___ / ___ / ___

Sleep _____ hrs

☐ ☐ ☐

Mood _____

☐ 🙁 ☐ 😐 ☐ 🙂

Caffeine ____ servings

☐ ☐ ☐

Favorite Places to Go to in Between Classes

Fuel	Chill	Study

Hobbies I Want to Keep Up on During the Quarter

My Thoughts

Rate My Day _____

Mood _____

☐ 🙁 ☐ 😐 ☐ 🙂

Stress Level _____

Today's Mission

Important Things

For School

Main Focus

Productive Breaks

Get Started

Get Ahead

For Myself

Main Focus

Stress-Free Tasks

Get Started

Personal Time

My Notes

Week 1

Friday

Today's Mantra for ___ / ___ / ___

Sleep _____ hrs

☐ ☐ ☐

Mood _____

☐ 😞 ☐ 😐 ☐ 🙂

Caffeine ____ servings

☐ ☐ ☐

How I'm Liking My Classes So Far

Course	Why I Like It
Rating: ○ ○ ○ ○ ○	....
Rating: ○ ○ ○ ○ ○	....
Rating: ○ ○ ○ ○ ○	....
Rating: ○ ○ ○ ○ ○	....
Rating: ○ ○ ○ ○ ○	....
Rating: ○ ○ ○ ○ ○	....
Rating: ○ ○ ○ ○ ○	....
Rating: ○ ○ ○ ○ ○	....

My Thoughts

Rate My Day _____

Mood _____

☐ 😞 ☐ 😐 ☐ 🙂

Stress Level _____

Today's Mission

Important Things

For School

Priority This Weekend

Start This Weekend

I'm Feeling Productive

Get Ahead

For Myself

Weekend Errands

Social Time

Surprise Myself

Personal Time

My Notes

Saturday

Sleep _____ hrs

Mood _____

Caffeine _____ servings

Good Memories This Week

Important Things I Learned This Week

from myself

from others

from school

My Thoughts

Rate My Day _____

Mood _____

Stress Level _____

Today's Mission

Important Things

For School

Start Easy

Catch Up On

Get Started On

Get Ahead

For Myself

For Confidence

For Fun

For Relaxation

Hobbies

My Notes

Week 1

Sunday

Today's Mantra for ___ / ___ / ___

Sleep _____ hrs

☐ ☐ ☐

Mood _____

☐ 😕 ☐ 😐 ☐ 😊

Caffeine ____ servings

☐ ☐ ☐

Ways I'm Going to Make Next Week Better

....
....
....
....
....

Goals for Next Week	Motivation
....	....
....	....
....	....
....	....
....	....
....	....
....	....
....	....
....	....
....	....
....	....

My Thoughts

Rate My Day _____

Mood _____

☐ 😕 ☐ 😐 ☐ 😊

Stress Level _____

Today's Mission

Important Things

For School

Redeem Myself

To Feel Proud

Only If Possible

For Myself

For Inspiration

For Positivity

For Self-Love

Get Ahead

Hobbies

My Notes

Week 2

/ - /

This Week's Goal

	Monday	Tuesday	Wednesday
Deadlines			
Events/Meetings			
Meals	☐ B ☐ L ☐ D	☐ B ☐ L ☐ D	☐ B ☐ L ☐ D
Exercise			

Goals	Plan of Action	Result/Reflection

Academic Habits	M	T	W	R	F	S	S	Personal Habits	M	T	W	R	F	S	S

How I Feel About My Classes?   1 *Behind*   2 *On Track*   3 *Ahead*   52

Course 1 ☐☐☐   Course 2 ☐☐☐   Course 3 ☐☐☐   Course 4 ☐☐☐

Course 5 ☐☐☐   Course 6 ☐☐☐   Course 7 ☐☐☐   Course 8 ☐☐☐

Thursday	Friday	Saturday

Sunday

☐ B   ☐ B   ☐ B   ☐ B
☐ L   ☐ L   ☐ L   ☐ L
☐ D   ☐ D   ☐ D   ☐ D

Academic	Extracurricular	Personal	Priorities

My Notes

Week 2

Monday

Sleep _____ hrs

Mood _____

Caffeine ____ servings

Getting Comfortable with Schedule	Getting Comfortable with Workload

Academic

Extracurricular

My Thoughts

Rate My Day _____

Mood _____

Stress Level _____

Today's Mission

Important Things

For School

Main Focus

Productive Breaks

Get Started

Get Ahead

For Myself

Main Focus

Stress-Free Tasks

Get Started

Personal Time

My Notes

Tuesday

Today's Mantra for   /   /

Sleep _____ hrs

Mood _____

Caffeine _____ servings

Instructor	Their Pet Peeves	Their Tips & Advice

My Thoughts

Rate My Day _____

Mood _____

Stress Level _____

Today's Mission

For School

Main Focus

Productive Breaks

Get Started

Get Ahead

For Myself

Main Focus

Stress-Free Tasks

Get Started

Personal Time

My Notes

Week 2
Wednesday

Today's Mantra for ___ / ___ / ___

Sleep _____ hrs

Mood _____

Caffeine _____ servings

My Current Energy	How to Maintain/Improve It
....	....
....	....
....	....
....	....
....	....
....	....
....	....
....	....

Anticipated Struggles This Quarter	Ways to Reframe the Problem
....	....
....	....
....	....
....	....
....	....
....	....
....	....
....	....

My Thoughts

Rate My Day _____

Mood _____

Stress Level _____

For School

Main Focus

Productive Breaks

Get Started

Get Ahead

For Myself

Main Focus

Stress-Free Tasks

Get Started

Personal Time

My Notes

Week 2

Thursday

Today's Mantra for ___ / ___ / ___

Sleep _____ hrs

☐ 👤 ☐ 👤 ☐ 👤 ᶻᶻᶻ

Mood _____

☐ 😟 ☐ 😐 ☐ 😊

Caffeine ____ servings

☐ ☕ ☐ 🍵 ☐ 🥤

Regular Tasks	Frequency	Time Needed

My Thoughts

Rate My Day _____

Mood _____

☐ 😟 ☐ 😐 ☐ 😊

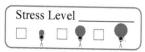

Stress Level _____

Today's Mission

Important Things

For School

Main Focus

Productive Breaks

Get Started

Get Ahead

For Myself

Main Focus

Stress-Free Tasks

Get Started

Personal Time

My Notes

Friday

Today's Mantra for ____ / ____ / ____

Sleep _____ hrs

Mood _____

Caffeine ____ servings

Highlights of School This Week

Ideas for Fun Adventures This Weekend

My Thoughts

Rate My Day _____

Mood _____

Stress Level _____

For School

Priority This Weekend

Start This Weekend

I'm Feeling Productive

Get Ahead

For Myself

Weekend Errands

Social Time

Surprise Myself

Personal Time

My Notes

Week 2

Saturday

Today's Mantra for   /   /

Sleep _____ hrs

Mood _____

Caffeine _____ servings

Good Memories This Week

Important Things I Learned This Week

from myself

from others

from school

My Thoughts

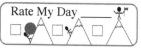

Rate My Day _____

Mood _____

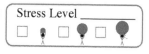

Stress Level _____

For School

Start Easy

Catch Up On

Get Started On

Get Ahead

For Myself

For Confidence

For Fun

For Relaxation

Hobbies

My Notes

Week 2

Sunday

Today's Mantra for ___ / ___ / ___

Sleep _____ hrs

Mood _____

Caffeine _____ servings

Ways I'm Going to Make Next Week Better

....

....

....

....

....

Goals for Next Week	Motivation

My Thoughts

Today's Mission

Important Things

For School

Redeem Myself

To Feel Proud

Only If Possible

For Myself

For Inspiration

For Positivity

For Self-Love

Get Ahead

Hobbies

My Notes

Midterms Study Plan

Midterm	Study Plan A ▪ ▪ ▪	Study Plan B ▪ ▪ ▪
Week / Day		
Course		
% of Grade		
comfort level: ○ ○ ○ ○ ○		

Midterm	Study Plan A ▪ ▪ ▪	Study Plan B ▪ ▪ ▪
Week / Day		
Course		
% of Grade		
comfort level: ○ ○ ○ ○ ○		

Midterm	Study Plan A ▪ ▪ ▪	Study Plan B ▪ ▪ ▪
Week / Day		
Course		
% of Grade		
comfort level: ○ ○ ○ ○ ○		

Midterm	Study Plan A ▪ ▪ ▪	Study Plan B ▪ ▪ ▪
Week / Day		
Course		
% of Grade		
comfort level: ○ ○ ○ ○ ○		

Midterm	Study Plan A ▪ ▪ ▪	Study Plan B ▪ ▪ ▪
Week / Day		
Course		
% of Grade		
comfort level: ○ ○ ○ ○ ○		

Midterm	Study Plan A ▪ ▪ ▪	Study Plan B ▪ ▪ ▪
Week / Day		
Course		
% of Grade		
comfort level: ○ ○ ○ ○ ○		

Midterm	Study Plan A ▪ ▪ ▪	Study Plan B ▪ ▪ ▪
Week / Day		
Course		
% of Grade		
comfort level: ○ ○ ○ ○ ○		

Midterm	Study Plan A ▪ ▪ ▪	Study Plan B ▪ ▪ ▪
Week / Day		
Course		
% of Grade		
comfort level: ○ ○ ○ ○ ○		

Week 3 - 5	The Big Day(s)

Week Goals	Monday	Tuesday	Wednesday
Week 3			
Anticipated Stress	○ ○ ○ ○ ○	○ ○ ○ ○ ○	○ ○ ○ ○ ○
Week 4			
Anticipated Stress	○ ○ ○ ○ ○	○ ○ ○ ○ ○	○ ○ ○ ○ ○
Week 5			
Anticipated Stress	○ ○ ○ ○ ○	○ ○ ○ ○ ○	○ ○ ○ ○ ○

Stressful Days	The Day Before	The Week Before

Inspiration From Myself	Inspiration From Others

Thursday	Friday	Saturday	Sunday

Continued Projects	Progress	Next Steps

New Projects	Steps	Progress/Reflection

Week 3

This Week's Goal

/ - /

	Monday	Tuesday	Wednesday
Deadlines			
Events/Meetings			
Meals	☐ B ☐ L ☐ D	☐ B ☐ L ☐ D	☐ B ☐ L ☐ D
Exercise			

Goals	Plan of Action	Result/Reflection

Academic Habits	M	T	W	R	F	S	S		Personal Habits	M	T	W	R	F	S	S

How I Feel About My Classes? 1 *Behind* 2 *On Track* 3 *Ahead*

Course 1 □□□   Course 2 □□□   Course 3 □□□   Course 4 □□□
Course 5 □□□   Course 6 □□□   Course 7 □□□   Course 8 □□□

Thursday

Friday

Saturday

Sunday

□ B
□ L
□ D

□ B
□ L
□ D

□ B
□ L
□ D

□ B
□ L
□ D

Academic	Extracurricular	Personal	Priorities

My Notes

Week 3

Monday

Sleep _____ hrs

Mood _____

Caffeine _____ servings

Things I'm Looking Forward To

....

....

....

....

....

....

....

....

My Favorite Inspirational Quotes

....

....

....

....

....

....

....

....

My Thoughts

Rate My Day _____

Mood _____

Stress Level _____

Today's Mission

Important Things

74

For School

Main Focus

Productive Breaks

Get Started

Study - Review - Prepare

For Myself

Main Focus

Stress-Free Tasks

Get Started

Personal Time

My Notes

Week 3

Tuesday

Today's Mantra for ___ / ___ / ___

Sleep _____ hrs

Mood _____

Caffeine ____ servings

How I Can Like My Classes More	
Course	Part(s) of the Curriculum That Intrigue Me
Rating: ○○○○○	
Rating: ○○○○○	
Rating: ○○○○○	
Rating: ○○○○○	
Rating: ○○○○○	
Rating: ○○○○○	
Rating: ○○○○○	
Rating: ○○○○○	

My Thoughts

Rate My Day _____

Mood _____

Stress Level _____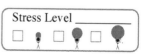

For School

Main Focus

Productive Breaks

Get Started

Study - Review - Prepare

For Myself

Main Focus

Stress-Free Tasks

Get Started

Personal Time

My Notes

Week 3

Wednesday

Today's Mantra for ____ / ____ / ____

Sleep _____ hrs

Mood _____

Caffeine _____ servings

Focus Needed	Tasks
Barely Any: *Quick & Easy*	
Here & There: *Brainstorming Needed*	
Full Presence: *Long Focused Time*	

Time Lost	That Time Repurposed
while waiting for classes to start	
while traveling to and from school	
while stuck on campus	

My Thoughts

Rate My Day _____

Mood _____

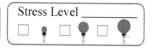

Stress Level _____

Today's Mission	Important Things	

For School

Main Focus

Productive Breaks

Get Started

Study - Review - Prepare

For Myself

Main Focus

Stress-Free Tasks

Get Started

Personal Time

My Notes

Thursday

Today's Mantra for   /   /

Sleep _____ hrs

Mood _____

Caffeine ____ servings

Transitional Times	Routines
morning routine	
getting back from classes	
after dinner	
night routine	

My Thoughts

Rate My Day _____

Mood _____

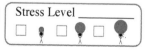

Stress Level _____

For School

Main Focus

Productive Breaks

Get Started

Study - Review - Prepare

For Myself

Main Focus

Stress-Free Tasks

Get Started

Personal Time

My Notes

Week 3

Friday

Sleep _____ hrs

☐ 🛏 ☐ 🛏 ☐ 🛏

Mood _____

☐ 😔 ☐ 😐 ☐ 😊

Caffeine _____ servings

☐ ☕ ☐ ☕ ☐ 🥤

Highlights of School This Week

....

....

....

....

....

....

....

....

Plan for a Relaxing Weekend

....

....

....

....

....

....

....

....

My Thoughts

Rate My Day _____

☐ ☐ ☐

Mood _____

☐ 😔 ☐ 😐 ☐ 😊

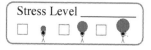

Stress Level _____

☐ 🎈 ☐ 🎈 ☐ 🎈

Today's Mission

Important Things

Priority This Weekend

For School

Start This Weekend

I'm Feeling Productive

Study - Review - Prepare

Weekend Errands

For Myself

Social Time

Surprise Myself

Personal Time

My Notes

Week 3

Saturday

Today's Mantra for   /   /

Sleep _____ hrs

Mood _____

Caffeine _____ servings

Good Memories This Week

How I Like My School - Life Balance

Things I've Done to Satisfy Others	Things I've Done to Satisfy Myself

My Thoughts

Rate My Day _____

Mood _____

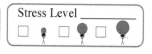
Stress Level _____

Today's Mission   Important Things   84

For School

Start Easy

Catch Up On

Get Started On

Study - Review - Prepare

For Myself

For Confidence

For Fun

For Relaxation

Hobbies

My Notes

Week 3
Sunday

Today's Mantra for ___ / ___ / ___

Sleep _____ hrs

Mood _____

Caffeine _____ servings

Ways I'm Going to Prepare Myself Mentally for Midterms

....

....

....

....

....

Goals for Next Week	Motivation
....	....
....	....
....	....
....	....
....	....
....	....
....	....
....	....
....	....
....	....
....	....

My Thoughts

Rate My Day _____

Mood _____

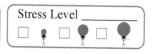
Stress Level _____

Today's Mission

Important Things

For School

Redeem Myself

To Feel Proud

Only If Possible

Study - Review - Prepare

For Myself

For Inspiration

For Positivity

For Self-Love

Hobbies

My Notes

Week 4	This Week's Goal

/ - /

Monday	Tuesday	Wednesday

Deadlines

Events/Meetings

Meals
- ☐ B
- ☐ L
- ☐ D

Meals
- ☐ B
- ☐ L
- ☐ D

Meals
- ☐ B
- ☐ L
- ☐ D

Exercise

Goals	Plan of Action	Result/Reflection

Academic Habits	M	T	W	R	F	S	S	Personal Habits	M	T	W	R	F	S	S

How I Feel About My Classes? 1 *Behind* 2 *On Track* 3 *Ahead*

Course 1 ☐☐☐   Course 2 ☐☐☐   Course 3 ☐☐☐   Course 4 ☐☐☐

Course 5 ☐☐☐   Course 6 ☐☐☐   Course 7 ☐☐☐   Course 8 ☐☐☐

Thursday	Friday	Saturday

Sunday

☐ B	☐ B	☐ B ☐ B
☐ L	☐ L	☐ L ☐ L
☐ D	☐ D	☐ D ☐ D

Academic	Extracurricular	Personal	
			Priorities

My Notes

Week 4

Monday

Today's Mantra for ____ / ____ / ____

Sleep _____ hrs

Mood _____

Caffeine ____ servings

Worries About Mid-Quarter Approaching

....
....
....
....
....

Obligations	Ways to Enjoy Them More
....	....
....	....
....	....
....	....
....	....
....	....
....	....
....	....
....	....
....	....

My Thoughts

Rate My Day _____

Mood _____

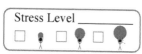

Stress Level _____

Today's Mission

Important Things

For School

Main Focus

Productive Breaks

Get Started

Study - Review - Prepare

For Myself

Main Focus

Stress-Free Tasks

Get Started

Personal Time

My Notes

Week 4

Tuesday

Today's Mantra for   /   /

Sleep _____ hrs
☐ ☐ ☐

Mood _____
☐ ☹ ☐ 😐 ☐ 🙂

Caffeine _____ servings
☐ ☐ ☐

Sources of Inspiration

....

....

....

....

....

Task I Don't Want to Do	What It's Keeping Me From
....	....
....	....
....	....
....	....
....	....
....	....
....	....
....	....
....	....
....	....
....	....

My Thoughts

Rate My Day _____

Mood _____
☐ ☹ ☐ 😐 ☐ 🙂

Stress Level _____

Today's Mission

Important Things

For School

Main Focus

Productive Breaks

Get Started

Study - Review - Prepare

For Myself

Main Focus

Stress-Free Tasks

Get Started

Personal Time

My Notes

Week 4
Wednesday

Today's Mantra for ___ / ___ / ___

Sleep _____ hrs

Mood _____

Caffeine _____ servings

Source of Busyness	Ways to Reallocate Time
....	....
....	....
....	....
....	....
....	....
....	....
....	....
....	....
....	....
....	....
....	....
....	....
....	....
....	....
....	....
....	....
....	....

My Thoughts

Rate My Day _____

Mood _____

Stress Level _____

Today's Mission

Important Things

For School

Main Focus

Productive Breaks

Get Started

Study - Review - Prepare

For Myself

Main Focus

Stress-Free Tasks

Get Started

Personal Time

My Notes

Week 4
Thursday

Sleep _____ hrs

Mood _____

Caffeine ____ servings

Study Task	Time Dedication	Study Plan
review notes		
organize concepts & details		
practice test (problems, or essays)		
review with others		

My Thoughts

Rate My Day _____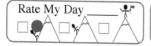

Mood _____

Stress Level _____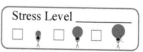

Today's Mission

Important Things

For School

Main Focus

Productive Breaks

Get Started

Study - Review - Prepare

For Myself

Main Focus

Stress-Free Tasks

Get Started

Personal Time

My Notes

Week 4

Friday

Sleep _____ hrs

Mood _____

Caffeine _____ servings

Highlights of School This Week

....

....

....

....

....

....

....

....

Plan for a Relaxing Weekend

....

....

....

....

....

....

....

....

My Thoughts

Rate My Day _____

Mood _____

Stress Level _____

For School

Priority This Weekend

Start This Weekend

I'm Feeling Productive

For Myself

Weekend Errands

Social Time

Surprise Myself

Study - Review - Prepare

Personal Time

My Notes

Week 4

Saturday

Sleep _____ hrs

Mood _____

Caffeine _____ servings

Good Memories This Week

Important Things I Learned This Week

from myself

from others

from school

My Thoughts

Rate My Day _____

Mood _____

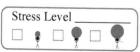

Stress Level _____

For School

Start Easy

Catch Up On

Get Started On

Study - Review - Prepare

For Myself

For Confidence

For Fun

For Relaxation

Hobbies

My Notes

Sunday

Today's Mantra for ___ / ___ / ___

Sleep _____ hrs

Mood _____

Caffeine ____ servings

Course	Approach Used	Analysis
		New Approach Needed? ☐Y ☐N
Effort Given: ○○○ *Priority Given:* ○○○		
		New Approach Needed? ☐Y ☐N
Effort Given: ○○○ *Priority Given:* ○○○		
		New Approach Needed? ☐Y ☐N
Effort Given: ○○○ *Priority Given:* ○○○		
		New Approach Needed? ☐Y ☐N
Effort Given: ○○○ *Priority Given:* ○○○		
		New Approach Needed? ☐Y ☐N
Effort Given: ○○○ *Priority Given:* ○○○		
		New Approach Needed? ☐Y ☐N
Effort Given: ○○○ *Priority Given:* ○○○		
		New Approach Needed? ☐Y ☐N
Effort Given: ○○○ *Priority Given:* ○○○		
		New Approach Needed? ☐Y ☐N
Effort Given: ○○○ *Priority Given:* ○○○		

My Thoughts

Rate My Day _____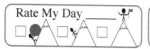

Mood _____

Stress Level _____

Today's Mission

Important Things

For School

Redeem Myself

To Feel Proud

Only If Possible

Study - Review - Prepare

For Myself

For Inspiration

For Positivity

For Self-Love

Hobbies

My Notes

Week 5

/ - /

This Week's Goal

Monday	Tuesday	Wednesday

Deadlines

Events/Meetings

Meals

Monday: ☐ B ☐ L ☐ D

Tuesday: ☐ B ☐ L ☐ D

Wednesday: ☐ B ☐ L ☐ D

Exercise

Goals	Plan of Action	Result/Reflection

Academic Habits	M	T	W	R	F	S	S	Personal Habits	M	T	W	R	F	S	S

How I Feel About My Classes? **1** *Behind* **2** *On Track* **3** *Ahead*

Course 1 ☐☐☐	Course 2 ☐☐☐	Course 3 ☐☐☐	Course 4 ☐☐☐
Course 5 ☐☐☐	Course 6 ☐☐☐	Course 7 ☐☐☐	Course 8 ☐☐☐

Thursday

Friday

Saturday

Sunday

☐ B
☐ L
☐ D

☐ B
☐ L
☐ D

☐ B
☐ L
☐ D

☐ B
☐ L
☐ D

Academic	Extracurricular	Personal	Priorities

My Notes

Monday

Today's Mantra for / /

Sleep _____ hrs

Mood _____

Caffeine _____ servings

Why I'm Overwhelmed

Stressor	Reverse the Impact
Stress Level: ○ ○ ○ ○ ○	mental:
	emotional:
	physical:
Stress Level: ○ ○ ○ ○ ○	mental:
	emotional:
	physical:
Stress Level: ○ ○ ○ ○ ○	mental:
	emotional:
	physical:
Stress Level: ○ ○ ○ ○ ○	mental:
	emotional:
	physical:

Mini - Adventure After Midterms/Deadlines This Week

My Thoughts

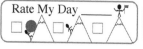

Rate My Day _____

Mood _____

Stress Level _____

Today's Mission

Important Things

For School

Main Focus

Productive Breaks

Get Started

Study - Review - Prepare

For Myself

Main Focus

Stress-Free Tasks

Get Started

Personal Time

My Notes

Week 5

Tuesday

Today's Mantra for ___ / ___ / ___

Sleep _____ hrs

Mood _____

Caffeine _____ servings

Low Effort Studying	Incorportion
	between classes:
	before bed:
	between classes:
	before bed:
	between classes:
	before bed:
	between classes:
	before bed:

High Effort Studying	Mental Breaks & Rewards

My Thoughts

Rate My Day _____

Mood _____

Stress Level _____

For School

Main Focus

Productive Breaks

Get Started

Study - Review - Prepare

For Myself

Main Focus

Stress-Free Tasks

Get Started

Recharge

My Notes

Wednesday

Sleep _____ hrs

Mood _____

Caffeine ____ servings

Reason for Procrastination	Ways to Combat
fear of *or* discomfort with task:	
perfectionism:	
difficult *or* overwhelming task:	
boring *or* tedious task:	

My Frustrations

Rate My Day _____

Mood _____

Stress Level _____

Today's Mission

Important Things

110

For School

Main Focus

Productive Breaks

Get Started

Study - Review - Prepare

For Myself

Main Focus

Stress-Free Tasks

Get Started

Catch a Break

My Notes

Week 5
Thursday

Today's Mantra for ___ / ___ / ___

Sleep _____ hrs

Mood _____

Caffeine _____ servings

Reminders That I'm Awesome

....
....
....
....
....

Review of Quarter Goals | Progress

My Thoughts

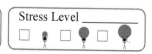

Today's Mission

Important Things

For School

Main Focus

Productive Breaks

Get Started

Study - Review - Prepare

For Myself

Main Focus

Stress-Free Tasks

Get Started

Treat Myself

My Notes

Week 5

Friday

Sleep _____ hrs
☐ 😴 ☐ 😴 ☐ 😴

Mood _____
☐ 😟 ☐ 😐 ☐ 😊

Caffeine _____ servings
☐ ☕ ☐ ☕ ☐ 🥤

Good Memories This Week

....
....
....
....
....

Study Plan This Weekend

Saturday

....
....
....
....
....

Sunday

....
....
....
....
....

My Thoughts

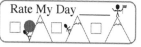

Rate My Day _____
☐ ☐ ☐

Mood _____
☐ 😟 ☐ 😐 ☐ 😊

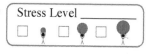

Stress Level _____
☐ ☐ ☐

Today's Mission

Important Things

For School

Priority This Weekend

Start This Weekend

I'm Feeling Productive

Study - Review - Prepare

For Myself

Weekend Errands

Social Time

Surprise Myself

Selfish Time

My Notes

Week 5

Saturday

Today's Mantra for ___ / ___ / ___

Sleep _____ hrs

☐ ☐ ☐

Mood _____

☐ 😔 ☐ 😐 ☐ 😊

Caffeine ____ servings

☐ ☐ ☐

Positive Moments This Week

Congratulate Myself on Halfway | Ways to Celebrate

My Thoughts

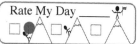

Rate My Day _____

☐ ☐ ☐

Mood _____

☐ 😔 ☐ 😐 ☐ 😊

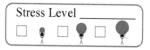

Stress Level _____

☐ ☐ ☐

Today's Mission

Important Things

For School

Start Easy

Catch Up On

Get Started On

Study - Review - Prepare

For Myself

For Confidence

For Fun

For Relaxation

Hobbies

My Notes

Week 5

Sunday

Today's Mantra for / /

Sleep _____ hrs

Mood _____

Caffeine _____ servings

How I Studied	Result & Analysis

Course
Effort Given: ○ ○ ○
Priority Given: ○ ○ ○
Review Notes: ○ ○ ○
Practice Skills: ○ ○ ○
Getting Help: ○ ○ ○

Course
Effort Given: ○ ○ ○
Priority Given: ○ ○ ○
Review Notes: ○ ○ ○
Practice Skills: ○ ○ ○
Getting Help: ○ ○ ○

Course
Effort Given: ○ ○ ○
Priority Given: ○ ○ ○
Review Notes: ○ ○ ○
Practice Skills: ○ ○ ○
Getting Help: ○ ○ ○

Course
Effort Given: ○ ○ ○
Priority Given: ○ ○ ○
Review Notes: ○ ○ ○
Practice Skills: ○ ○ ○
Getting Help: ○ ○ ○

Course
Effort Given: ○ ○ ○
Priority Given: ○ ○ ○
Review Notes: ○ ○ ○
Practice Skills: ○ ○ ○
Getting Help: ○ ○ ○

Course
Effort Given: ○ ○ ○
Priority Given: ○ ○ ○
Review Notes: ○ ○ ○
Practice Skills: ○ ○ ○
Getting Help: ○ ○ ○

Course
Effort Given: ○ ○ ○
Priority Given: ○ ○ ○
Review Notes: ○ ○ ○
Practice Skills: ○ ○ ○
Getting Help: ○ ○ ○

Course
Effort Given: ○ ○ ○
Priority Given: ○ ○ ○
Review Notes: ○ ○ ○
Practice Skills: ○ ○ ○
Getting Help: ○ ○ ○

My Thoughts

Rate My Day _____

Mood _____

Stress Level _____

Today's Mission

Important Things

Redeem Myself

For School

To Feel Proud

Only If Possible

Study - Review - Prepare

For Inspiration

For Myself

For Positivity

For Self-Love

Hobbies

My Notes

Midterms Study Plan

Midterm	Study Plan A ▪ ▪ ▪	Study Plan B ▪ ▪ ▪
Week / Day Course % of Grade comfort level: ○ ○ ○ ○ ○		

Midterm	Study Plan A ▪ ▪ ▪	Study Plan B ▪ ▪ ▪
Week / Day Course % of Grade comfort level: ○ ○ ○ ○ ○		

Midterm	Study Plan A ▪ ▪ ▪	Study Plan B ▪ ▪ ▪
Week / Day Course % of Grade comfort level: ○ ○ ○ ○ ○		

Midterm	Study Plan A ▪ ▪ ▪	Study Plan B ▪ ▪ ▪
Week / Day Course % of Grade comfort level: ○ ○ ○ ○ ○		

Midterm	**Study Plan A** ▪ ▪ ▪	**Study Plan B** ▪ ▪ ▪
Week / Day		
Course		
% of Grade		
comfort level: ○ ○ ○ ○ ○		

Midterm	**Study Plan A** ▪ ▪ ▪	**Study Plan B** ▪ ▪ ▪
Week / Day		
Course		
% of Grade		
comfort level: ○ ○ ○ ○ ○		

Midterm	**Study Plan A** ▪ ▪ ▪	**Study Plan B** ▪ ▪ ▪
Week / Day		
Course		
% of Grade		
comfort level: ○ ○ ○ ○ ○		

Midterm	**Study Plan A** ▪ ▪ ▪	**Study Plan B** ▪ ▪ ▪
Week / Day		
Course		
% of Grade		
comfort level: ○ ○ ○ ○ ○		

Week 6 - 8	The Big Day(s)

Week Goals	Monday	Tuesday	Wednesday
Week 6			
Anticipated Stress ○ ○ ○ ○ ○	○ ○ ○ ○ ○	○ ○ ○ ○ ○	○ ○ ○ ○ ○
Week 7			
Anticipated Stress ○ ○ ○ ○ ○	○ ○ ○ ○ ○	○ ○ ○ ○ ○	○ ○ ○ ○ ○
Week 8			
Anticipated Stress ○ ○ ○ ○ ○	○ ○ ○ ○ ○	○ ○ ○ ○ ○	○ ○ ○ ○ ○

Stressful Days	The Day Before	The Week Before

Inspiration From Myself	Inspiration From Others

Thursday	Friday	Saturday	Sunday

Continued Projects	Progress	Next Steps

New Projects	Steps	Progress/Reflection

Week 6

/ - /

Monday	Tuesday	Wednesday

Deadlines

Events/Meetings

Meals

- Monday: ☐ B ☐ L ☐ D
- Tuesday: ☐ B ☐ L ☐ D
- Wednesday: ☐ B ☐ L ☐ D

Exercise

Goals	Plan of Action	Result/Reflection

Academic Habits	M	T	W	R	F	S	S

Personal Habits	M	T	W	R	F	S	S

Course 1 [ ][ ][ ]   Course 2 [ ][ ][ ]   Course 3 [ ][ ][ ]   Course 4 [ ][ ][ ]
Course 5 [ ][ ][ ]   Course 6 [ ][ ][ ]   Course 7 [ ][ ][ ]   Course 8 [ ][ ][ ]

Thursday	Friday	Saturday
		Sunday

Thursday:
☐ B
☐ L
☐ D

Friday:
☐ B
☐ L
☐ D

Saturday:
☐ B
☐ L
☐ D

Sunday:
☐ B
☐ L
☐ D

Academic	Extracurricular	Personal	Priorities

My Notes

Week 6
Monday

Sleep _____ hrs

Mood _____

Caffeine ____ servings

Why I'm Overwhelmed

Stressor	Reverse the Impact
Stress Level: ○ ○ ○ ○ ○	mental:
	emotional:
	physical:
Stress Level: ○ ○ ○ ○ ○	mental:
	emotional:
	physical:
Stress Level: ○ ○ ○ ○ ○	mental:
	emotional:
	physical:
Stress Level: ○ ○ ○ ○ ○	mental:
	emotional:
	physical:

How I'm Going to Treat Myself This Weekend

My Thoughts

Rate My Day _____

Mood _____

Stress Level _____

Today's Mission

Important Things

For School

Main Focus

Productive Breaks

Get Started

For Myself

Main Focus

Stress-Free Tasks

Get Started

Study - Review - Prepare

Personal Time

My Notes

Week 6

Tuesday

Today's Mantra for _____ / _____ / _____

Sleep _____ hrs

Mood _____

Caffeine _____ servings

Recent Successes

Current Distractions | Reasons They Can Wait

My Thoughts

Rate My Day _____

Mood _____

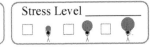

Stress Level _____

Today's Mission

Important Things

For School

Main Focus

Productive Breaks

Get Started

Study - Review - Prepare

For Myself

Main Focus

Stress-Free Tasks

Get Started

Recharge

My Notes

Week 6

Wednesday

Today's Mantra for ____/____/____

Sleep _____ hrs

Mood _____

Caffeine ____ servings

Study Task	Mental Break Ideas
Mental Effort: ○ ○ ○ ○ ○ No. of Breaks: _____	
Mental Effort: ○ ○ ○ ○ ○ No. of Breaks: _____	
Mental Effort: ○ ○ ○ ○ ○ No. of Breaks: _____	
Mental Effort: ○ ○ ○ ○ ○ No. of Breaks: _____	
Mental Effort: ○ ○ ○ ○ ○ No. of Breaks: _____	
Mental Effort: ○ ○ ○ ○ ○ No. of Breaks: _____	
Mental Effort: ○ ○ ○ ○ ○ No. of Breaks: _____	
Mental Effort: ○ ○ ○ ○ ○ No. of Breaks: _____	

My Frustrations

Rate My Day _____

Mood _____

Stress Level _____

Main Focus	**For School**

Productive Breaks	

Get Started	

Main Focus	**For Myself**

Stress-Free Tasks	

Get Started	

Study - Review - Prepare

Catch a Break

My Notes

Week 6

Thursday

Sleep _____ hrs

Mood _____

Caffeine _____ servings

How Much Better I Am at Dealing with Stress

Frustrations	Reframing the Problem

My Thoughts

Rate My Day _____

Mood _____

Stress Level _____

Main Focus

For School

For Myself

Productive Breaks

Stress-Free Tasks

Get Started

Get Started

Study - Review - Prepare

Treat Myself

My Notes

Week 6

Friday

Today's Mantra for ___ / ___ / ___

Sleep _____ hrs

☐ 🛏 ☐ 🛏 ☐ 🛏

Mood _____

☐ 😞 ☐ 😐 ☐ 😊

Caffeine ____ servings

☐ ☕ ☐ ☕ ☐ 🥤

How I've Exceeded My Expectations

attitude

....
....
....
....
....

work ethic

....
....
....
....

staying relaxed

....
....
....
....
....

My Thoughts

Rate My Day _____

Mood _____

☐ 😞 ☐ 😐 ☐ 😊

Stress Level _____

For School

Priority This Weekend

Start This Weekend

I'm Feeling Productive

Study - Review - Prepare

For Myself

Weekend Errands

Social Time

Surprise Myself

Selfish Time

My Notes

Week 6

Saturday

Sleep _____ hrs

Mood _____

Caffeine _____ servings

Positive Moments This Week

What I've Learned About Myself

strengths

studying style

memory tricks

My Thoughts

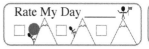

Rate My Day _____

Mood _____

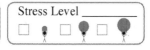

Stress Level _____

Today's Mission

Important Things

For School

Start Easy

Catch Up On

Get Started On

Study - Review - Prepare

For Myself

For Confidence

For Fun

For Relaxation

Hobbies

My Notes

Week 6

Sunday

Today's Mantra for ___/___/___

Sleep _____ hrs

Mood _____

Caffeine _____ servings

How I'm Going to Balance Studying & Recharging

How I'm Going to Make Next Week More:

time-efficient

relaxed

enjoyable

My Thoughts

Rate My Day _____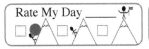

Mood _____

Stress Level _____

For School

Redeem Myself

To Feel Proud

Only If Possible

Study - Review - Prepare

For Myself

For Inspiration

For Positivity

For Self-Love

Hobbies

My Notes

This Week's Goal

Monday	Tuesday	Wednesday

Deadlines

Events/Meetings

Meals

Monday: ☐ B ☐ L ☐ D
Tuesday: ☐ B ☐ L ☐ D
Wednesday: ☐ B ☐ L ☐ D

Exercise

Goals	Plan of Action	Result/Reflection

Academic Habits	M	T	W	R	F	S	S	Personal Habits	M	T	W	R	F	S	S

Course 1 [ ][ ][ ]   Course 2 [ ][ ][ ]   Course 3 [ ][ ][ ]   Course 4 [ ][ ][ ]

Course 5 [ ][ ][ ]   Course 6 [ ][ ][ ]   Course 7 [ ][ ][ ]   Course 8 [ ][ ][ ]

Thursday	Friday	Saturday
		Sunday

☐ B   ☐ B   ☐ B   ☐ B
☐ L   ☐ L   ☐ L   ☐ L
☐ D   ☐ D   ☐ D   ☐ D

Academic	Extracurricular	Personal	Priorities

My Notes

Week 7

Monday

Sleep _____ hrs

Mood _____

Caffeine _____ servings

Responsibility	Why I'm Doing It	Ways to Recharge
Satisfaction: ○ ○ ○ Break Needed? ☐Y ☐N		
Satisfaction: ○ ○ ○ Break Needed? ☐Y ☐N		
Satisfaction: ○ ○ ○ Break Needed? ☐Y ☐N		
Satisfaction: ○ ○ ○ Break Needed? ☐Y ☐N		
Satisfaction: ○ ○ ○ Break Needed? ☐Y ☐N		
Satisfaction: ○ ○ ○ Break Needed? ☐Y ☐N		
Satisfaction: ○ ○ ○ Break Needed? ☐Y ☐N		
Satisfaction: ○ ○ ○ Break Needed? ☐Y ☐N		

My Thoughts

Rate My Day _____

Mood _____

Stress Level _____

Today's Mission

Important Things

For School

Main Focus

For Myself

Main Focus

Productive Breaks

Stress-Free Tasks

Get Started

Get Started

Study - Review - Prepare

Personal Time

My Notes

Tuesday

Sleep _____ hrs

Mood _____

Caffeine _____ servings

Ways I've Changed for the Better This Quarter

self-love

....
....
....
....
....
....

skill set

....
....
....
....
....
....

how I treat others

....
....
....
....
....
....

My Thoughts

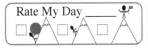

Rate My Day _____

Mood _____

Stress Level _____

For School

Main Focus

Productive Breaks

Get Started

Study - Review - Prepare

For Myself

Main Focus

Stress-Free Tasks

Get Started

Recharge

My Notes

Wednesday

Today's Mantra for ____ / ____ / ____

Sleep _____ hrs

Mood _____

Caffeine _____ servings

Habits that Eat My Time	Habits That Will Conserve Time

My Frustrations

Rate My Day _____

Mood _____

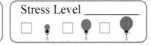

Stress Level _____

For School

For Myself

Main Focus

Main Focus

Productive Breaks

Stress-Free Tasks

Get Started

Get Started

Study - Review - Prepare

Catch a Break

My Notes

Week 7

Thursday

Sleep _____ hrs

Mood _____

Caffeine _____ servings

Goals	Currently Doing	Next Steps

My Thoughts

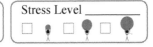

Today's Mission

Important Things

For School

Main Focus

Productive Breaks

Get Started

Study - Review - Prepare

For Myself

Main Focus

Stress-Free Tasks

Get Started

Treat Myself

My Notes

Week 7

Friday

Today's Mantra for ___ / ___ / ___

Sleep _____ hrs

Mood _____

Caffeine ____ servings

Times I Was Going to Give Up But Didn't

Cool Facts I Learned This Quarter

My Thoughts

Rate My Day _____

Mood _____

Stress Level _____

Today's Mission

Important Things

Priority This Weekend

For School

Start This Weekend

I'm Feeling Productive

Study - Review - Prepare

Weekend Errands

For Myself

Social Time

Surprise Myself

Selfish Time

My Notes

Week 7

Saturday

Today's Mantra for ___ / ___ / ___

Sleep _____ hrs

Mood _____

Caffeine ____ servings

Positive Moments This Week

Things I Learned From My Instructors

My Thoughts

Rate My Day _____

Mood _____

Stress Level _____

Today's Mission

Important Things

For School

Start Easy

Catch Up On

Get Started On

Study - Review - Prepare

For Myself

For Confidence

For Fun

For Relaxation

Hobbies

My Notes

Week 7

Sunday

Today's Mantra for ___/___/___

Sleep _____ hrs

Mood _____

Caffeine _____ servings

How I Studied		Result & Analysis
Course _____	Effort Given: ○○○ Priority Given: ○○○ Review Notes: ○○○ Practice Skills: ○○○ Getting Help: ○○○	
Course _____	Effort Given: ○○○ Priority Given: ○○○ Review Notes: ○○○ Practice Skills: ○○○ Getting Help: ○○○	
Course _____	Effort Given: ○○○ Priority Given: ○○○ Review Notes: ○○○ Practice Skills: ○○○ Getting Help: ○○○	
Course _____	Effort Given: ○○○ Priority Given: ○○○ Review Notes: ○○○ Practice Skills: ○○○ Getting Help: ○○○	
Course _____	Effort Given: ○○○ Priority Given: ○○○ Review Notes: ○○○ Practice Skills: ○○○ Getting Help: ○○○	
Course _____	Effort Given: ○○○ Priority Given: ○○○ Review Notes: ○○○ Practice Skills: ○○○ Getting Help: ○○○	
Course _____	Effort Given: ○○○ Priority Given: ○○○ Review Notes: ○○○ Practice Skills: ○○○ Getting Help: ○○○	
Course _____	Effort Given: ○○○ Priority Given: ○○○ Review Notes: ○○○ Practice Skills: ○○○ Getting Help: ○○○	

My Thoughts

Rate My Day _____

Mood _____

Stress Level _____

Today's Mission	Important Things	154

For School

Redeem Myself

To Feel Proud

Only If Possible

For Myself

For Inspiration

For Positivity

For Self-Love

Study - Review - Prepare

Hobbies

My Notes

Week 8

/ - /

This Week's Goal

Monday	Tuesday	Wednesday

Deadlines

Events/Meetings

Meals

Monday:
- B
- L
- D

Tuesday:
- B
- L
- D

Wednesday:
- B
- L
- D

Exercise

Goals	Plan of Action	Result/Reflection

Academic Habits	M	T	W	R	F	S	S	Personal Habits	M	T	W	R	F	S	S

Course 1 ☐☐☐   Course 2 ☐☐☐   Course 3 ☐☐☐   Course 4 ☐☐☐
Course 5 ☐☐☐   Course 6 ☐☐☐   Course 7 ☐☐☐   Course 8 ☐☐☐

Thursday

Friday

Saturday

Sunday

☐ B
☐ L
☐ D

☐ B
☐ L
☐ D

☐ B
☐ L
☐ D

☐ B
☐ L
☐ D

Academic	Extracurricular	Personal	
			Priorities

My Notes

Week 8

Monday

Today's Mantra for ___/___/___

Sleep _____ hrs

Mood _____

Caffeine ____ servings

Negative Aspects of Classes	Regaining Control of My Experience

My Thoughts

Rate My Day _____

Mood _____

Stress Level _____

Today's Mission

Important Things

For School

Main Focus

Productive Breaks

Get Started

Study - Review - Prepare

For Myself

Main Focus

Stress-Free Tasks

Get Started

Personal Time

My Notes

Week 8

Tuesday

Sleep _____ hrs

Mood _____

Caffeine _____ servings

Course/Extracurricular	How It Fits into the Bigger Picture

My Thoughts

Rate My Day _____

Mood _____

Stress Level _____

For School

Main Focus

Productive Breaks

Get Started

Study - Review - Prepare

For Myself

Main Focus

Stress-Free Tasks

Get Started

Recharge

My Notes

Week 8

Wednesday

Today's Mantra for ___ / ___ / ___

Sleep _____ hrs

Mood _____

Caffeine _____ servings

How I'm Going to Stay on Track

Current Distractions	Reasons They Can Wait

My Frustrations

Rate My Day _____

Mood _____

Stress Level _____

For School

Main Focus

Productive Breaks

Get Started

Study - Review - Prepare

For Myself

Main Focus

Stress-Free Tasks

Get Started

Catch a Break

My Notes

Week 8

Thursday

Today's Mantra for ____ / ____ / ____

Sleep _____ hrs

Mood _____

Caffeine ____ servings

Current Situation	Best Case Scenario	Actions to Take

My Thoughts

Rate My Day _____

Mood _____

Stress Level _____

For School

Main Focus

Productive Breaks

Get Started

For Myself

Main Focus

Stress-Free Tasks

Get Started

Study - Review - Prepare

Treat Myself

My Notes

Week 8

Friday

Sleep _____ hrs

Mood _____

Caffeine _____ servings

Things I Didn't Think I Could Do But Still Did Well

....

....

....

....

....

Setbacks	Forgiveness

My Thoughts

Rate My Day _____

Mood _____

Stress Level _____

Today's Mission

Important Things

For School

Priority This Weekend

Start This Weekend

I'm Feeling Productive

Study - Review - Prepare

For Myself

Weekend Errands

Social Time

Surprise Myself

Selfish Time

My Notes

Week 8

Saturday

Sleep _____ hrs

Mood _____

Caffeine _____ servings

Positive Moments This Week

What I've Learned About How I Like to Study

what works

what doesn't work

effective rewards

My Thoughts

Rate My Day _____

Mood _____

Stress Level _____

Today's Mission

Important Things

For School

Start Easy

Catch Up On

Get Started On

Study - Review - Prepare

For Myself

For Confidence

For Fun

For Relaxation

Hobbies

My Notes

Week 8

Sunday

Today's Mantra for ___ / ___ / ___

Sleep _____ hrs

Mood _____

Caffeine ____ servings

How I'm Going to Stay Motivated Until the End

....
....
....
....
....
....
....
....

How I'm Going to Stay Relaxed Next Week

....
....
....
....
....
....
....
....

My Thoughts

Rate My Day _____

Mood _____

Stress Level _____

Today's Mission

Important Things

For School

Redeem Myself

To Feel Proud

Only If Possible

For Myself

For Inspiration

For Positivity

For Self-Love

Study - Review - Prepare

Hobbies

My Notes

Week 9 - Finals	The Big Day(s)

Week Goals	Monday	Tuesday	Wednesday
Week 9			
Anticipated Stress	○ ○ ○ ○ ○	○ ○ ○ ○ ○	○ ○ ○ ○ ○
Week 10			
Anticipated Stress	○ ○ ○ ○ ○	○ ○ ○ ○ ○	○ ○ ○ ○ ○
Finals Week			
Anticipated Stress	○ ○ ○ ○ ○	○ ○ ○ ○ ○	○ ○ ○ ○ ○

Stressful Days	The Day Before	The Week Before

Inspiration From Myself	Inspiration From Others

Thursday	Friday	Saturday	Sunday

Continued Projects	Progress	Next Steps

New Projects	Steps	Progress/Reflection

Week 9

This Week's Goal

/ - /

Monday	Tuesday	Wednesday

Deadlines

Events/Meetings

Meals

☐ B ☐ L ☐ D

☐ B ☐ L ☐ D

☐ B ☐ L ☐ D

Exercise

Goals	Plan of Action	Result/Reflection

Academic Habits	M	T	W	R	F	S	S	Personal Habits	M	T	W	R	F	S	S

Course 1 ☐☐☐   Course 2 ☐☐☐   Course 3 ☐☐☐   Course 4 ☐☐☐
Course 5 ☐☐☐   Course 6 ☐☐☐   Course 7 ☐☐☐   Course 8 ☐☐☐

Thursday

Friday

Saturday

Sunday

☐ B   ☐ B   ☐ B   ☐ B
☐ L   ☐ L   ☐ L   ☐ L
☐ D   ☐ D   ☐ D   ☐ D

Academic	Extracurricular	Personal	Priorities

My Notes

Week 9

Monday

Sleep _____ hrs

Mood _____

Caffeine ____ servings

Worries for End of Quarter	Reassurance Based on Facts

My Thoughts

Rate My Day _____

Mood _____

Stress Level _____

Today's Mission

Important Things

For School

Main Focus

Productive Breaks

Get Started

Study - Review - Prepare

For Myself

Main Focus

Stress-Free Tasks

Get Started

Personal Time

My Notes

Tuesday

Today's Mantra for ___ / ___ / ___

Sleep _____ hrs

Mood _____

Caffeine _____ servings

Inspirational People & Experiences

Qualities I Admire in Myself

My Thoughts

Rate My Day _____

Mood _____

Stress Level _____

For School

Main Focus

Productive Breaks

Get Started

Study - Review - Prepare

For Myself

Main Focus

Stress-Free Tasks

Get Started

Recharge

My Notes

Week 9

Wednesday

Sleep _____ hrs

Mood _____

Caffeine ____ servings

What Instructor Likes to Test On	Preparation & Test Taking Strategies

My Frustrations

Rate My Day _____

Mood _____

Stress Level _____

For School

Main Focus

Productive Breaks

Get Started

Study - Review - Prepare

For Myself

Main Focus

Stress-Free Tasks

Get Started

Catch a Break

My Notes

Week 9

Thursday

Sleep _____ hrs

Mood _____

Caffeine _____ servings

Regrets & Mistakes	Acceptance & Moving On

My Thoughts

Rate My Day _____

Mood _____

Stress Level _____

For School

Main Focus

Productive Breaks

Get Started

Study - Review - Prepare

For Myself

Main Focus

Stress-Free Tasks

Get Started

Treat Myself

My Notes

Friday

Today's Mantra for   /   /

Sleep _____ hrs

Mood _____

Caffeine _____ servings

Positive Ways I Surprised Myself

Cool Facts I Learned This Quarter

My Thoughts

Rate My Day _____

Mood _____

Stress Level _____

Today's Mission   Important Things

For School

Priority This Weekend

Start This Weekend

I'm Feeling Productive

For Myself

Weekend Errands

Social Time

Surprise Myself

Study - Review - Prepare

Selfish Time

My Notes

Saturday

Today's Mantra for   /   /

Sleep _____ hrs

Mood _____

Caffeine _____ servings

Positive Moments This Week

New Skills I Acquired This Quarter

My Thoughts

Rate My Day _____

Mood _____

Stress Level _____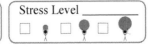

Today's Mission

Important Things

For School

Start Easy

Catch Up On

Get Started On

Study - Review - Prepare

For Myself

For Confidence

For Fun

For Relaxation

Hobbies

My Notes

Week 9

Sunday

Today's Mantra for ___/___/___

Sleep _____ hrs

Mood _____

Caffeine ____ servings

Study Goals for Finals	Motivation

My Thoughts

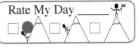 Rate My Day _____

 Mood _____

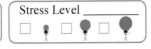 Stress Level _____

Today's Mission

Important Things

For School

Redeem Myself

To Feel Proud

Only If Possible

For Myself

For Inspiration

For Positivity

For Self-Love

Study - Review - Prepare

Hobbies

My Notes

Finals Study Plan

Make several study plans for each final.
Evaluate to prioritize & motivate studying.

Final:

Idealistic	Realistic	Last Minute

Importance ○ ○ ○ ○ ○   *Contentment* ○ ○ ○ ○ ○   *Risk* ○ ○ ○ ○ ○

Final:

Idealistic	Realistic	Last Minute

Importance ○ ○ ○ ○ ○   *Contentment* ○ ○ ○ ○ ○   *Risk* ○ ○ ○ ○ ○

Idealistic	Realistic	Last Minute

Importance ○ ○ ○ ○ ○   Contentment ○ ○ ○ ○ ○   Risk ○ ○ ○ ○ ○

Final:

Idealistic	Realistic	Last Minute

Importance ○ ○ ○ ○ ○   Contentment ○ ○ ○ ○ ○   Risk ○ ○ ○ ○ ○

Final:

Finals Study Plan

Idealistic	Realistic	Last Minute

Importance ○ ○ ○ ○ ○   Contentment ○ ○ ○ ○ ○   Risk ○ ○ ○ ○ ○

Final:

Idealistic	Realistic	Last Minute

Importance ○ ○ ○ ○ ○   Contentment ○ ○ ○ ○ ○   Risk ○ ○ ○ ○ ○

Final:

Idealistic	Realistic	Last Minute

Importance ○ ○ ○ ○ ○   *Contentment* ○ ○ ○ ○ ○   *Risk* ○ ○ ○ ○ ○

Final:

Idealistic	Realistic	Last Minute

Importance ○ ○ ○ ○ ○   *Contentment* ○ ○ ○ ○ ○   *Risk* ○ ○ ○ ○ ○

Final:

Week 10

/ - /

	Monday	Tuesday	Wednesday
Deadlines			
Events/Meetings			
Meals	☐ B ☐ L ☐ D	☐ B ☐ L ☐ D	☐ B ☐ L ☐ D
Exercise			

Goals	Plan of Action	Result/Reflection

Academic Habits	M	T	W	R	F	S	S	Personal Habits	M	T	W	R	F	S	S

How I Feel About My Classes? 1 *Behind* 2 *On Track* 3 *Ahead*   194

Course 1 ☐☐☐   Course 2 ☐☐☐   Course 3 ☐☐☐   Course 4 ☐☐☐
Course 5 ☐☐☐   Course 6 ☐☐☐   Course 7 ☐☐☐   Course 8 ☐☐☐

Thursday	Friday	Saturday

Sunday

☐ B   ☐ B   ☐ B   ☐ B
☐ L   ☐ L   ☐ L   ☐ L
☐ D   ☐ D   ☐ D   ☐ D

Academic	Extracurricular	Personal	Priorities

My Notes

Week 10

Monday

Today's Mantra for ___/___/___

Sleep _____ hrs

Mood _____

Caffeine ____ servings

Reasons Why It's Not the End of the World

How I'm Going to Make the Best of Things

My Thoughts

Rate My Day _____

Mood _____

Stress Level _____

Today's Mission

Important Things

Main Focus

For School

Productive Breaks

Get Started

Study - Review - Prepare

Main Focus

For Myself

Stress-Free Tasks

Get Started

Personal Time

My Notes

Tuesday

Today's Mantra for   /   /

Sleep _____ hrs

Mood _____

Caffeine _____ servings

Skills I Have That Will Allow Me to Achieve the Unimaginable

....

....

....

....

....

....

....

....

....

Successes, Big or Small, This Quarter

....

....

....

....

....

....

....

....

....

My Thoughts

Rate My Day _____

Mood _____

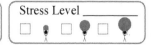

Stress Level _____

For School

Main Focus

Productive Breaks

Get Started

Study - Review - Prepare

For Myself

Main Focus

Stress-Free Tasks

Get Started

Recharge

My Notes

Week 10
Wednesday

Today's Mantra for   /   /

Sleep _____ hrs

Mood _____

Caffeine _____ servings

How I'm Going to Make Up for Lost Time

Strategies for Effective Studying for Each Class

1

5

2

6

3

7

4

8

My Frustrations

Rate My Day _____

Mood _____

Stress Level _____

Today's Mission | Important Things |

For School

Main Focus

Productive Breaks

Get Started

Study - Review - Prepare

For Myself

Main Focus

Stress-Free Tasks

Get Started

Catch a Break

My Notes

Thursday

Today's Mantra for ____ / ____ / ____

Sleep _____ hrs

Mood _____

Caffeine ____ servings

Hardest Concepts to Remember	Relation to My Interests

My Thoughts

Rate My Day _____

Mood _____

Stress Level _____

For School

Main Focus

Productive Breaks

Get Started

Study - Review - Prepare

For Myself

Main Focus

Stress-Free Tasks

Get Started

Treat Myself

My Notes

Week 10
Friday

Today's Mantra for ___/___/___

Sleep _____ hrs

Mood _____

Caffeine _____ servings

Proudest Moments This Quarter

Preparation for Finals

healthy meals

enough rest

relaxation

My Thoughts

Rate My Day _____

Mood _____

Stress Level _____

Today's Mission

Important Things

For School

Priority This Weekend

Start This Weekend

I'm Feeling Productive

Study - Review - Prepare

For Myself

Weekend Errands

Social Time

Surprise Myself

Selfish Time

My Notes

Week 10

Saturday

Today's Mantra for ___ / ___ / ___

Sleep _____ hrs

Mood _____

Caffeine ____ servings

Best Memories This Quarter

Positive Results of This Quarter

My Thoughts

Rate My Day _____

Mood _____

Stress Level _____

For School

Start Easy

Catch Up On

Get Started On

Study - Review - Prepare

For Myself

For Confidence

For Fun

For Relaxation

Hobbies

My Notes

Week 10

Sunday

Sleep _____ hrs

Mood _____

Caffeine _____ servings

How I'm Going to Mentally Prepare for Each Final

1	5
2	6
3	7
4	8

Compatible Subjects to Alternate Studying

My Thoughts

Rate My Day _____

Mood _____

Stress Level _____

For School

Redeem Myself

To Feel Proud

Only If Possible

For Myself

For Inspiration

For Positivity

For Self-Love

Study - Review - Prepare

Hobbies

My Notes

Study Week *or* Deadweek

/ - /

This Week's Goal

	Monday	Tuesday	Wednesday
Review Sessions			
Additional Office Hours			
Meals	☐ B ☐ L ☐ D	☐ B ☐ L ☐ D	☐ B ☐ L ☐ D
Exercise			

Questions to Ask During Review Sessions

Course 1 ☐☐☐   Course 2 ☐☐☐   Course 3 ☐☐☐   Course 4 ☐☐☐

Course 5 ☐☐☐   Course 6 ☐☐☐   Course 7 ☐☐☐   Course 8 ☐☐☐

Thursday

Friday

Saturday

Sunday

☐ B
☐ L
☐ D

☐ B
☐ L
☐ D

☐ B
☐ L
☐ D

☐ B
☐ L
☐ D

Questions to Ask During Additional Office Hours

Study Week

Monday

Today's Mission for   /   /

Studying

(Re)Learn

Breaks

Fuel !!

Study

Mental Breaks

Review

Movement

Concepts I'm Confident On

Relaxation

My Notes

Tuesday

Studying	Breaks

(Re)Learn — Studying

Fuel !! — Breaks

Study

Mental Breaks

Review

Movement

Concepts I'm Confident On	Relaxation

My Notes

Wednesday

Today's Mission for   /   /

Studying

(Re)Learn

Study

Review

Concepts I'm Confident On

Breaks

Fuel !!

Mental Breaks

Movement

Relaxation

My Notes

Thursday

Studying

(Re)Learn

Breaks

Fuel !!

Study

Mental Breaks

Review

Movement

Concepts I'm Confident On

Relaxation

My Notes

Friday

Today's Mantra for   /   /

Sleep _____ hrs

Mood _____

Caffeine _____ servings

Fundamentals	Main Concepts	Important Details

Final:

comfort level ○ ○ ○ ○ ○   *comfort level* ○ ○ ○ ○ ○   *comfort level* ○ ○ ○ ○ ○

Fundamentals	Main Concepts	Important Details

Final:

comfort level ○ ○ ○ ○ ○   *comfort level* ○ ○ ○ ○ ○   *comfort level* ○ ○ ○ ○ ○

Rate My Day _____

Mood _____

Stress Level _____

Studying

(Re)Learn

Study

Review

Concepts I'm Confident On

Breaks

Fuel !!

Mental Breaks

Movement

Relaxation

My Notes

Saturday

Today's Mantra for   /   /

Sleep _____ hrs

Mood _____

Caffeine _____ servings

Fundamentals	Main Concepts	Important Details

Final:

comfort level ○ ○ ○ ○ ○   comfort level ○ ○ ○ ○ ○   comfort level ○ ○ ○ ○ ○

Fundamentals	Main Concepts	Important Details

Final:

comfort level ○ ○ ○ ○ ○   comfort level ○ ○ ○ ○ ○   comfort level ○ ○ ○ ○ ○

Rate My Day _____

Mood _____

Stress Level _____

Today's Mission

Important Things

218

Studying

(Re)Learn

Study

Review

Concepts I'm Confident On

Breaks

Fuel !!

Mental Breaks

Movement

Relaxation

My Notes

Study Week

Sunday

Today's Mantra for ___ / ___ / ___

Sleep _____ hrs
☐ ☐ ☐

Mood _____
☐ 😟 ☐ 😐 ☐ 😊

Caffeine ____ servings
☐ ☐ ☐

Fundamentals	Main Concepts	Important Details

comfort level ○ ○ ○ ○ ○   *comfort level* ○ ○ ○ ○ ○   *comfort level* ○ ○ ○ ○ ○

Final:

Fundamentals	Main Concepts	Important Details

comfort level ○ ○ ○ ○ ○   *comfort level* ○ ○ ○ ○ ○   *comfort level* ○ ○ ○ ○ ○

Final:

Rate My Day _____
☐ ☐ ☐

Mood _____
☐ 😟 ☐ 😐 ☐ 😊

Stress Level _____
☐ ☐ ☐

Today's Mission

Important Things

Studying

(Re)Learn

Study

Review

Concepts I'm Confident On

Breaks

Fuel !!

Mental Breaks

Movement

Relaxation

My Notes

Finals Week

/ - /

This Week's Goal

	Monday	Tuesday	Wednesday
Finals			
Top Priority Studying			
Meals	☐ B ☐ L ☐ D	☐ B ☐ L ☐ D	☐ B ☐ L ☐ D
Exercise			

Worries	Reassurance

Course 1 | | | | Course 2 | | | | Course 3 | | | | Course 4 | | | |

Course 5 | | | | Course 6 | | | | Course 7 | | | | Course 8 | | | |

Thursday

Friday

Light Down the Tunnel

Retail* Therapy

* or Food

☐ B
☐ L
☐ D

☐ B
☐ L
☐ D

☐ I made it !!
☐ The Quarter is behind me now!
☐ I am proud of my hard work!

Proudest Moment of the Quarter:

(Re)Learn	Study	Review	
			Studying Priorities

Monday

Today's Mantra for ___ / ___ / ___

Sleep _____ hrs

Mood _____

Caffeine _____ servings

Fundamentals	Main Concepts	Important Details

Final:

comfort level ○ ○ ○ ○ ○   comfort level ○ ○ ○ ○ ○   comfort level ○ ○ ○ ○ ○

Fundamentals	Main Concepts	Important Details

Final:

comfort level ○ ○ ○ ○ ○   comfort level ○ ○ ○ ○ ○   comfort level ○ ○ ○ ○ ○

Rate My Day _____

Mood _____

Stress Level _____

Studying

(Re)Learn

Study

Review

Concepts I'm Confident On

Breaks

Fuel !!

Mental Breaks

Movement

Relaxation

My Notes

Tuesday

Today's Mantra for   /   /

Sleep _____ hrs

Mood _____

Caffeine _____ servings

Fundamentals	Main Concepts	Important Details

Final:

comfort level ○ ○ ○ ○ ○   comfort level ○ ○ ○ ○ ○   comfort level ○ ○ ○ ○ ○

Fundamentals	Main Concepts	Important Details

Final:

comfort level ○ ○ ○ ○ ○   comfort level ○ ○ ○ ○ ○   comfort level ○ ○ ○ ○ ○

Rate My Day _____

Mood _____

Stress Level _____

Studying

(Re)Learn

Study

Review

Breaks

Fuel !!

Mental Breaks

Movement

Concepts I'm Confident On

Relaxation

My Notes

Finals Week
Wednesday

Today's Mantra for   /   /

Sleep _____ hrs

Mood _____

Caffeine _____ servings

Fundamentals	Main Concepts	Important Details

Final:

comfort level ○ ○ ○ ○ ○   comfort level ○ ○ ○ ○ ○   comfort level ○ ○ ○ ○ ○

Fundamentals	Main Concepts	Important Details

Final:

comfort level ○ ○ ○ ○ ○   comfort level ○ ○ ○ ○ ○   comfort level ○ ○ ○ ○ ○

Rate My Day _____

Mood _____

Stress Level _____

Today's Mission

Important Things

Studying

(Re)Learn

Study

Review

Breaks

Fuel !!

Mental Breaks

Movement

Concepts I'm Confident On

Relaxation

My Notes

Finals Week

Thursday

Today's Mantra for ___ / ___ / ___

Sleep _____ hrs

Mood _____

Caffeine _____ servings

Fundamentals	Main Concepts	Important Details

Final:

comfort level ○ ○ ○ ○ ○   comfort level ○ ○ ○ ○ ○   comfort level ○ ○ ○ ○ ○

Fundamentals	Main Concepts	Important Details

Final:

comfort level ○ ○ ○ ○ ○   comfort level ○ ○ ○ ○ ○   comfort level ○ ○ ○ ○ ○

Rate My Day _____

Mood _____

Stress Level _____

Studying

(Re)Learn

Study

Review

Concepts I'm Confident On

Breaks

Fuel !!

Mental Breaks

Movement

Relaxation

My Notes

Friday

Today's Mantra for ___ / ___ / ___

Sleep _____ hrs

Mood _____

Caffeine _____ servings

Fundamentals	Main Concepts	Important Details

Final:

comfort level ○ ○ ○ ○ ○   comfort level ○ ○ ○ ○ ○   comfort level ○ ○ ○ ○ ○

Fundamentals	Main Concepts	Important Details

Final:

comfort level ○ ○ ○ ○ ○   comfort level ○ ○ ○ ○ ○   comfort level ○ ○ ○ ○ ○

Rate My Day _____

Mood _____

Stress Level _____

Studying

(Re)Learn

Study

Review

Breaks

Fuel !!

Mental Breaks

Movement

Concepts I'm Confident On

Relaxation

My Notes

End of Quarter Reflection

Reflect to make next quarter better!

	What I Did Well This Quarter	What I Could Have Done Better
Academic		
Extracurricular		
Personal		

Made in the USA
San Bernardino, CA
01 October 2015